Hustling and Bustling
CRANES

WHEELS AND
~~TOMOBILES~~

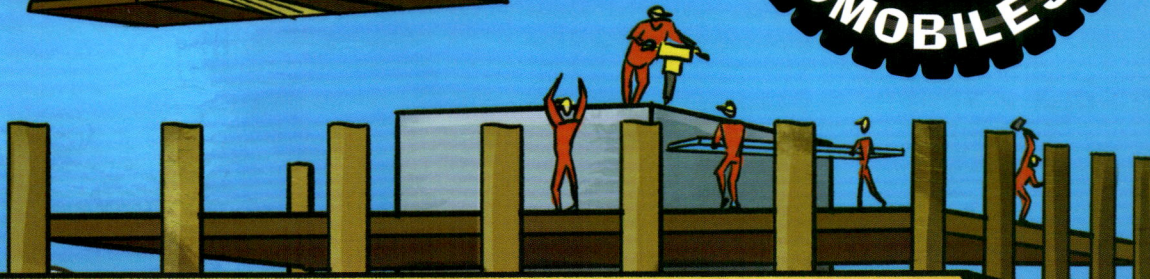

FOX EYE
PUBLISHING

A crane is a very clever machine.
It lifts and moves heavy things like a dream.

A crane lifts a load high above the ground.
Then it turns around and puts the load down.

Most cranes are for lifting and moving things around.

But cranes that have a wrecking ball knock buildings to the ground!

oil rig

Some cranes that work at ports
and oil rigs float upon the sea.

Some cranes crawl along on tracks.
Some cranes move on wheels.

Some cranes are on trucks that move the crane around.

The cranes that move the heaviest things are fixed down to the ground.

Tower cranes are the tallest.
They are eight storeys tall.

How many cranes can you see in this picture?
Can you count them all?

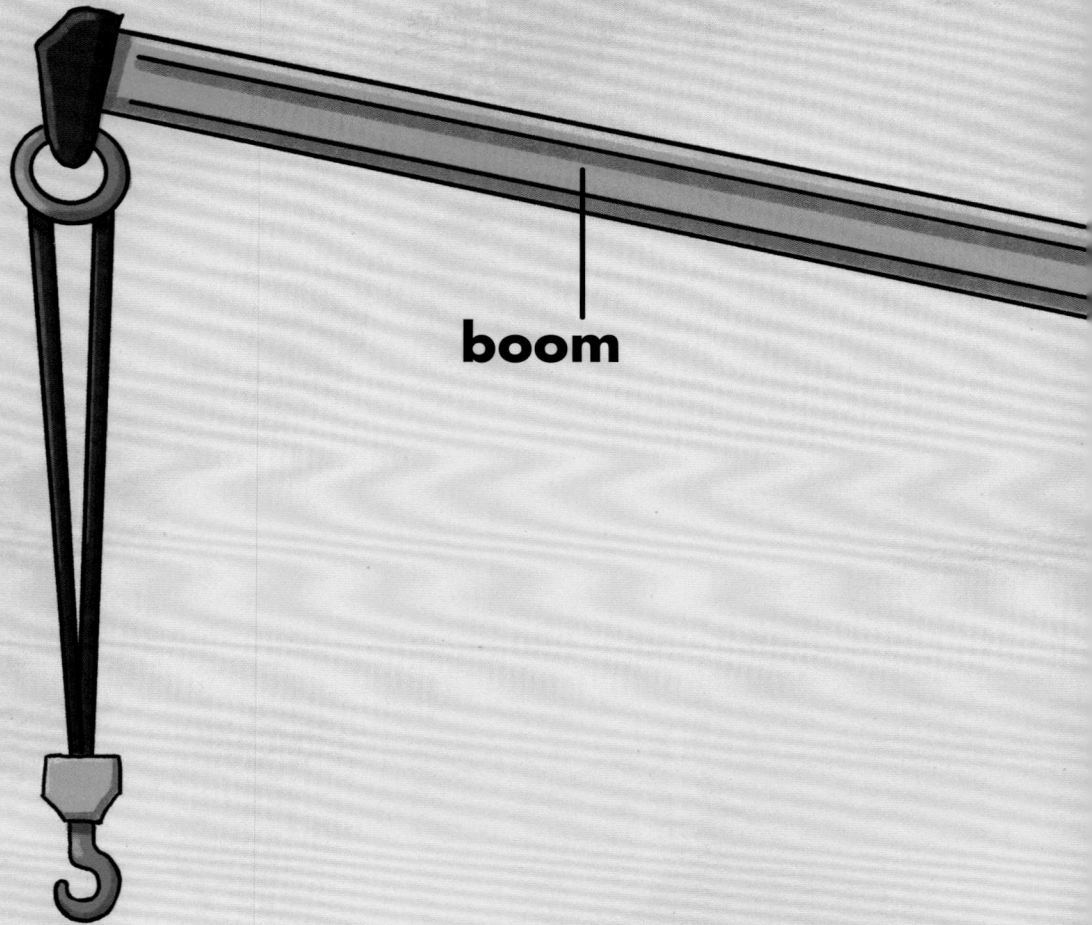

boom

All cranes have an engine.
It gives them the power to move.

They also have a long, strong arm.
It is called a boom.

cable

container

hook

A ship is coming into port.
Its containers of goods are piled high.

With its strong cable and huge hook,
the crane lifts one into the sky.

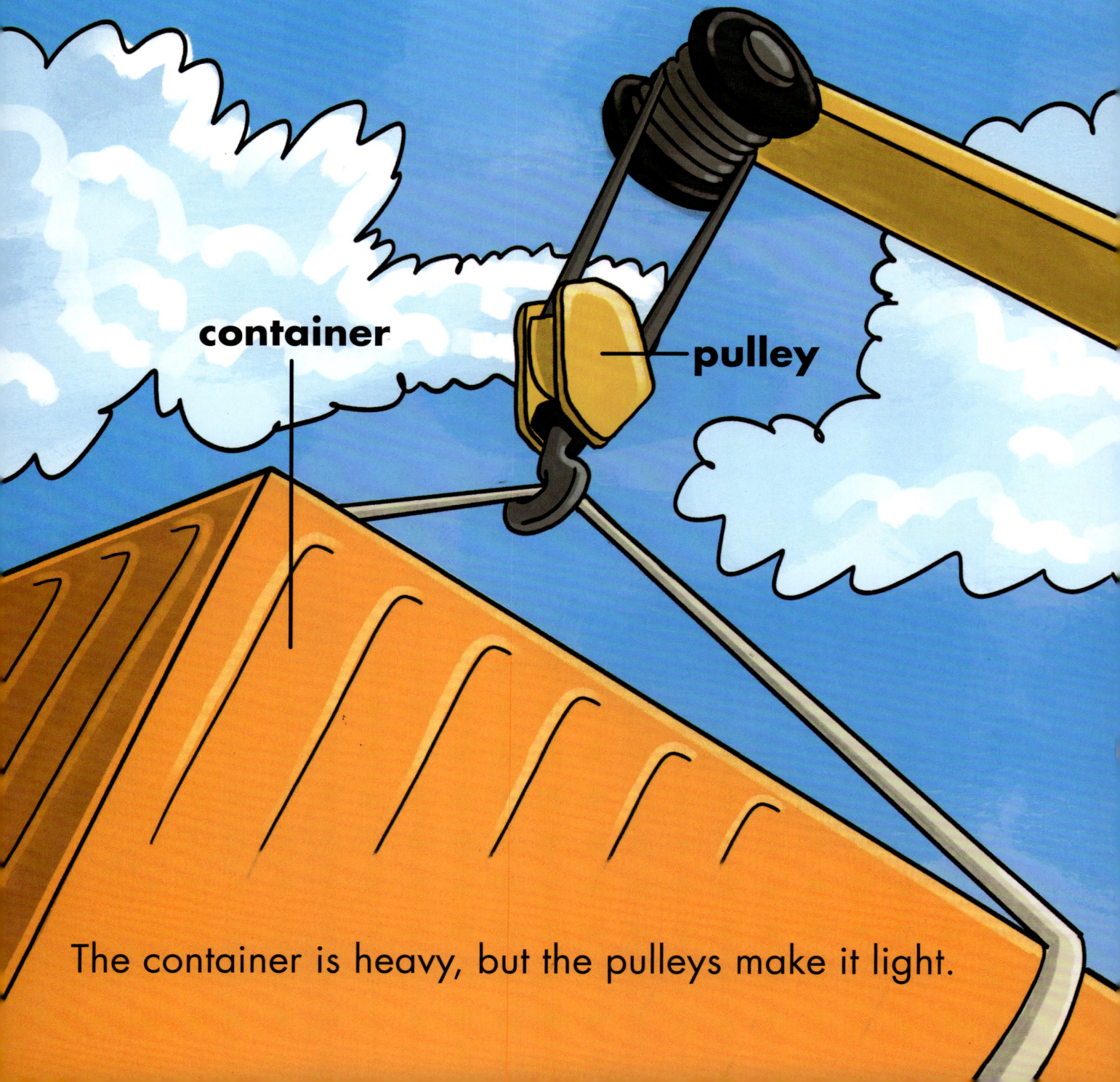

container

pulley

The container is heavy, but the pulleys make it light.

The crane is designed to stay balanced and upright.

An outrigger keeps the crane stable on the ground.

outrigger

It stops the base from moving as the crane turns around.

The container is lowered onto a truck that will carry it on the road.

truck

At last, the truck arrives at its final stop where it will unload.

Bustling Words

Balanced means to be even.

The **base** is the bottom of something.

A **cable** is a long piece of wire.

Containers hold things, such as goods.

Designed means made in a certain way.

An **engine** is part of a machine that makes its energy.

A **load** is something that is lifted.

A **machine** helps us to do work.

An **outrigger** is a leg on the base of a crane. It stops the crane from tipping over.

A **port** is a place that ships and boats sail into and sail from.

Power is energy to do something.

Pulleys are fixed wheels that have grooves. Cables run through the grooves. They are attached to heavy things. Pulleys are used to make lifting heavy things easier.

Storeys are the levels, or floors, of buildings.

Tower cranes are very tall cranes that are used to lift things up high.

Unload means to take a load off a vehicle.

First published in 2024 by Fox Eye Publishing
Unit 31, Vulcan House Business Centre,
Vulcan Road, Leicester, LE5 3EF
www.foxeyepublishing.com

Author: Katherine Eason
Art director: Paul Phillips
Cover designer: Emma Bailey
Editor: Jenny Rush

All illustrations by Eszter Szepvolgyi

978-1-80445-339-1

Printed in China